Mini Treats

igloobooks

Published in 2013
by Igloo Books Ltd
Cottage Farm
Sywell
NN6 0BJ
www.igloobooks.com

Copyright© 2013 Igloo Books Ltd

Food photography and recipe development: PhotoCuisine UK
Front and back cover images © PhotoCuisine UK

HUN001 0813
2 4 6 8 10 9 7 5 3 1
ISBN 978-1-78197-434-6

Printed and manufactured in China

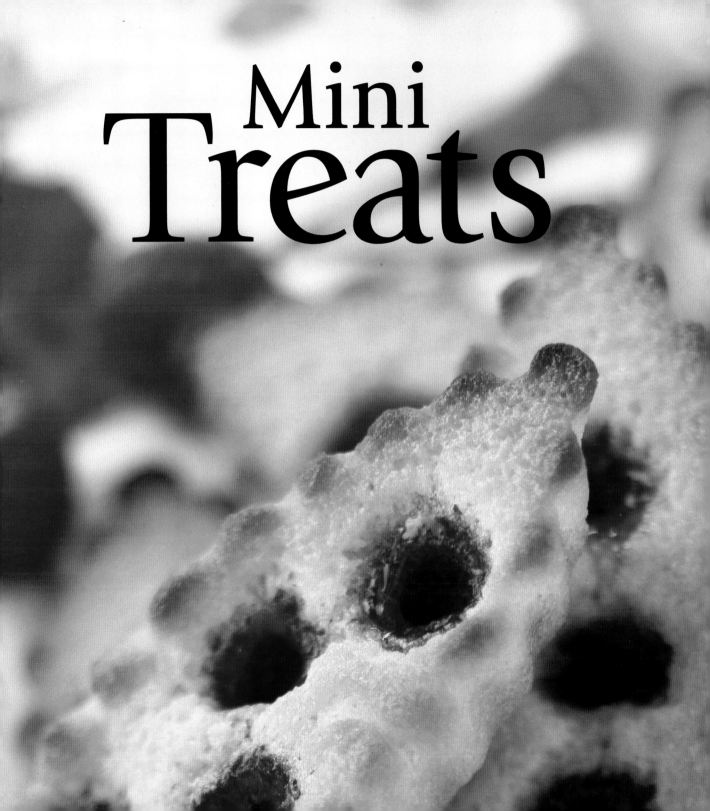

Mini
Treats

Contents

Everyday

Mushroom Burgers

Ingredients

450 g / 1 lb / 3 cups beef mince

16 large button mushrooms, stems removed

1 onion, finely sliced

1 beef tomato, sliced

a small handful of baby spinach leaves

4 slices of cheese, quartered

salt and pepper

Method

Preheat the oven to 190°C (170° fan) / 375F / gas 5.

Mix the beef mince with seasoning in a mixing bowl before dividing in 8 and shaping into mini patties.

Arrange the patties on a greaseproof paper-lined baking tray and bake for 10-12 minutes until coloured all over.

Remove from the oven and pat dry using kitchen paper.

Turn half of the button mushrooms upside down and layer a few spinach leaves, then slices of onion and tomato.

Top with the patties, then a piece of cheese and finally the remaining mushrooms.

Sprinkle the tops with sesame seeds before serving.

Serves: **4**   Preparation time: **10-15 minutes**   Cooking time: **15-20 minutes**

Gingerbread Tartlets

Ingredients

250 g / 9 oz ready-made sweet shortcrust pastry

a little plain (all purpose) flour, for dusting

225 g / 8 oz / 2 cups ground almonds

110 g / 4 oz / ⅓ cup treacle, warmed

110 g / 4 oz / ½ cup unsalted butter, softened

2 small eggs

2 small egg whites

2 tsp ground ginger

55 g / 2 oz / ½ cup assorted crystallised fruits

Method

Preheat the oven to 180°C (160° fan) / 350F / gas 4.

Roll the pastry out on a lightly floured surface to ½ cm thickness.

Cut out pastry rounds and use to line an assortment of 6 different shaped tartlet moulds.

Prick the bases with a fork and trim any excess, overhanging pastry.

Blitz together the ground almonds, ground ginger, treacle and butter in a food processor until creamy.

Add the eggs and egg whites, pulsing until combined.

Spoon into the pastry and dot with assorted candied fruit.

Bake for 20-25 minutes until the edge of the pastry is golden brown in colour and the filling is puffed slightly.

Remove to a wire rack to cool before turning out and serving.

Serves: **4**   Preparation time: **10 minutes**   Cooking time: **15-20 minutes**

Cod Fritters

Ingredients

For the fritters:
1 l / 1 pint 16 fl. oz / 4 cups groundnut oil

300 g / 10 ½ oz / 2 cup salt cod, rinsed in cold water overnight

75 g / 3 oz / ½ cup plain (all purpose) flour

For the batter:
110 g / 4 oz / ⅔ cup self-raising flour

125 ml / 4 ½ fl. oz / ½ cup cold water

1 red chilli (chili), deseeded and finely chopped

a small handful of flat-leaf parsley, finely chopped

salt and pepper

a few sprigs of flat-leaf parsley

½ tsp flaked sea salt

Method

Heat the groundnut oil in a large, heavy-based saucepan until hot; you can tell when the oil is hot enough as bubbles appear on a wooden spoon dipped in the hot oil.

Briefly whisk together the self-raising flour, chilli, chopped parsley, water and seasoning until you have a rough batter.

Dry the salt cod really well before mashing with 1 tbsp of plain flour and a little pepper in a mixing bowl.

Shape into small nuggets and dust in the remaining plain flour, shaking off any excess.

Dip in the batter and deep-fry in batches until golden-brown in colour all over; 2-3 minutes.

Remove with a slotted spoon to kitchen paper.

Serve in paper cones with a sprinkling of sea salt and a garnish of flat-leaf parsley.

Serves: 4   Preparation time: **10-15 minutes**   Cooking time: **15-20 minutes**

Chocolate and Toffee Tartlets

Ingredients

250 g / 9 oz ready-made shortcrust pastry

a little plain (all purpose) flour, for dusting

250 g / 9 oz / 1 ⅔ cups good-quality dark chocolate, chopped

250 ml / 9 fl. oz / 1 cup double (heavy) cream

75 g / 3 oz / ⅓ cup dulce de leche

2 medium eggs

Method

Preheat the oven to 180°C (160° fan) / 350F / gas 4.

Roll the pastry out on a lightly floured surface to ½ cm thickness.

Cut out 4 rounds of pastry and use to line 4 individual 4 inch fluted tartlet cases.

Prick the bases with a fork and trim any excess, overhanging pastry.

Line with greaseproof paper and fill with baking beans before blind-baking for 12-15 minutes until golden at the edges.

Remove from the oven and discard the greaseproof paper and baking beans.

Return to the oven for 3-4 minutes to brown the base before removing to a wire rack to cool.

Melt the cream and chocolate together in a heatproof bowl set atop a saucepan of simmering water, stirring occasionally.

Remove from the saucepan once melted and leave to cool 3 minutes before beating in the eggs.

Let the chocolate mixture cool and thicken lightly before pouring into the pastry cases and topping with a generous tablespoon of dulce de leche.

Serves: **4**   Preparation time: **10 minutes**   Cooking time: **20 minutes**

Omelette Brochettes

Ingredients

55 ml / 2 fl. oz / ¼ cup olive oil

250 ml / 9 fl. oz / 1 cup whole milk

12 large eggs

1 onion, finely chopped

1 red chilli (chili) pepper, deseeded and finely diced

a small handful of flat-leaf parsley leaves, finely chopped

salt and pepper

30 ml / 1 fl. oz / 2 tbsp extra-virgin olive oil

a small handful of flat-leaf parsley, finely chopped

Method

Preheat the oven to 180°C (160° fan) / 350F / gas 4.

Grease and line a 7 inch square cake tin with greaseproof paper.

Heat the olive oil in a frying pan set over a medium heat until hot.

Sweat the onion and chilli pepper with a little salt until the onion is translucent.

Whisk together the eggs and milk with a generous amount of seasoning in a separate bowl.

Stir in the onion and chilli followed by the parsley.

Pour into the cake tin and bake for 10-12 minutes until the egg is set.

Remove from the oven and allow to cool in the tin before turning out and cutting into squares.

Skewer 4 squares together and arrange on a serving plate.

Stir together the chopped parsley and olive oil for garnishing before drizzling on top of the Omelette Brochettes.

Serves: 4   Preparation time: **10 minutes**   Cooking time: **10-15 minutes**

Fresh Raspberry Financiers

Ingredients

110 g / 4 oz / ½ cup caster (superfine) sugar

110 g / 4 oz / ½ cup slightly salted butter, softened

1 tbsp unsalted butter, softened

110 g / 4 oz / 1 cup ground almonds

30 g / 1 oz / 2 tbsp plain (all purpose) flour, sifted

3 medium egg whites

a pinch of salt

200 g / 7 oz / 2 cups raspberries

Method

Brown the butter in a saucepan until nutty in aroma.

Strain through a fine sieve into a clean bowl, allowing it to cool.

Combine the flour, almonds and sugar in a mixing bowl.

Gently whisk the egg whites into this mixture and then fold through the cooled, melted butter.

Chill for 30 minutes.

Preheat the oven to 180°C (160° fan) / 350F / gas 4.

Grease a 12-hole fluted financier tin with unsalted butter.

Arrange 4 raspberries in each mould before pouring in the batter.

Bake for 15-18 minutes until golden brown at the edges and risen.

Remove to a wire rack to cool before turning out and serving.

Makes: **12**   Preparation time: **10 minutes**   Cooking time: **15 minutes**

Prawns Coated in Grated Coconut

Ingredients

1 l / 1 pint 16 fl. oz / 4 cups groundnut oil, for deep-frying

12 large raw prawns (shrimps)

2 medium eggs, beaten

150 g / 5 oz / 1 cup grated or desiccated coconut

50 g / 2 oz / ⅓ cup plain (all purpose) flour

salt and pepper

1 lime, sliced

a few banana leaves

Method

Heat the groundnut oil in a large, heavy-based saucepan until hot; you can tell when the oil is hot enough as bubbles appear on a wooden spoon dipped in the hot oil.

Season the flour and coat the prawns in it, shaking off any excess.

Dip in the egg and coat well in the coconut before arranging on a lined baking tray.

Deep-fry in batches until golden-brown in colour and crisp all over; 3-4 minutes usually.

Remove with a slotted spoon and drain on kitchen paper.

Line serving glasses with banana leaves and slices of lime before tucking the prawns in them and serving.

Serves: **4**   Preparation time: **5-10 minutes**   Cooking time: **10-15 minutes**

Sweet Pistachio Cookies

Ingredients

300 g / 10 ½ oz / 2 cups plain
(all purpose) flour

a little extra plain (all purpose) flour,
for dusting

50 g / 2 oz / ⅓ cup cornflour (cornstarch)

225 g / 8 oz / 1 cup unsalted butter, cubed

110 g / 4 oz / 1 cup shelled pistachios

75 g / 3 oz / 1 cup icing (confectioners')
sugar

30 g / 1 oz / 2 tbsp caster (superfine) sugar

Method

Pulse together the flour, cornflour, salt, icing sugar and butter in a food processor until it comes together to form a dough.

Remove the dough, knead gently and form into a ball.

Wrap in clingfilm and chill for 60 minutes.

Preheat the oven to 180°C (160° fan) / 350F / gas 4.

Pulse the pistachios and caster sugar together in a food processor until ground.

Remove the dough from the fridge and divide into two.

Roll both pieces out to 1 cm thickness on a lightly floured surface.

Sprinkle the chopped pistachio mixture on top of one piece of the dough then carefully lift the other piece of dough on top, sealing well.

Cut out 12 rounds using an embossed cookie cutter and arrange on a greaseproof paper-lined baking tray.

Bake for 15-18 minutes until the cookies are golden in colour on top.

Remove to a wire rack to cool before dusting with icing sugar.

Makes: **12**   Preparation time: **10-15 minutes**   Cooking time: **20 minutes**

Salmon and Dill Mini Loaves

Ingredients

250 g / 9 oz / 1 ⅔ cups self-raising flour, sifted

125 ml / 4 ½ fl. oz / ½ cup olive oil

110 g / 4 oz / 1 cup Parmesan cheese, finely grated

2 skinless salmon fillets, diced

1 tbsp black poppy seeds

1 tsp dried dill

2 large eggs, beaten

salt and pepper

a few sprigs of dill

Method

Preheat the oven to 170°C (150°C fan) / 325°F / gas 3.

Grease and line 6 mini loaf tins with greaseproof paper.

Whisk together the eggs and olive oil in a jug.

Combine the flour, salmon, dried dill and Parmesan cheese in a mixing bowl.

Add the wet ingredients to the dry ones and fold until combined.

Add some seasoning before spooning into the loaf tins and sprinkling the tops with poppy seeds.

Bake for 40-50 minutes; test with a wooden toothpick, if it comes out clean, the cakes are done.

Remove from the oven and leave to cool before turning out, slicing and garnishing with dill.

Makes: **6**   Preparation time: **10 minutes**   Cooking time: **10-15 minutes**

Mini Lime Cheesecakes

Ingredients

150 g / 5 oz / 1 cup shortbread biscuits, pulsed into fine crumbs

50 g / 2 oz / ¼ cup unsalted butter, melted

400 g / 14 oz / 2 cups cream cheese

250 g / 9 oz / 1 cup Greek yoghurt

110 g / 4 oz / ½ cup caster (superfine) sugar

2 sheets of gelatine

2 limes, juiced and finely zested

2 tbsp cold water

1 lime, finely zested

Method

Mix together the shortbread and melted butter until they resemble wet sand.

Press into the base of 4 mini springform cheesecake moulds and chill.

Beat together the cream cheese and sugar in a mixing bowl for 2 minutes until smooth and creamy.

Soften the gelatin in 2 tablespoons of lime juice and the cold water, then heat in a small saucepan to dissolve the gelatin.

Add the Greek yoghurt to the cream cheese mixture, beat well then add the gelatin mixture and beat again thoroughly.

Add the remaining lime juice and the zest, beating well before spooning on top of the biscuit base in the moulds.

Tap lightly to release any trapped air bubbles.

Cover and chill for 2 hours.

When ready to serve, run a warm, wet palette knife around the inside edge of the ramekins and turn out onto serving plates.

Garnish the tops with lime zest before serving.

Makes: **4**   Preparation time: **10-15 minutes**   Cooking time: **20 minutes**

Sun-dried Tomato and Rocket Pizzas

Ingredients

For the pizza dough:
300 g / 11 oz / 2 cups wheat flour

120 ml / 4 fl. oz / ½ cup warm water

20 g / ¾ oz of yeast

2 tbsp olive oil

For the topping:
1 tbsp pine nuts

110 g / 4 oz / ½ cup passata

75 g / 3 oz / ¾ cup Parmesan cheese

75 g / 3 oz / ½ cup sun-dried tomatoes

a small handful of rocket (arugula)

1 tbsp olive oil

salt and pepper

Method

Put the flour in a bowl, form a hole and crumble in the yeast and add the salt. Combine with warm water and form a ball.

Let it rest for 15 minutes in a warm place. Add olive oil and work the dough again. Form a ball again and cover it with flour. Wrap in a towel and let it rest for 15 minutes.

Preheat the oven to 200°C (180° fan) / 400F / gas 6.

Divide the dough into 8 small balls and roll out on a lightly floured surface to 3 inches in diameter.

Arrange on baking trays and drizzle with a little olive oil.

Spread a teaspoon of passata on top, then follow with a few pine nuts and some Sun-dried tomatoes.

Bake for 10-12 minutes until the dough is risen and cooked.

Remove from the oven and top with some rocket leaves and shaved Parmesan cheese before serving.

Makes: **8**   Preparation time: **10 minutes**   Cooking time: **10-15 minutes**

Chocolate and Hazelnut Tartlets

Ingredients

250 g / 9 oz ready-made shortcrust pastry

a little plain (all purpose) flour, for dusting

250 g / 9 oz / 1 ⅔ cups good-quality dark chocolate, chopped

110 g / 4 oz / ½ cup unsalted butter, cubed

110 ml / 4 fl. oz / ½ cup double (heavy) cream

55 g / 2 oz / ⅓ cup hazelnuts (cob nuts)

150 g / 5 oz / 2/3 cup caster (superfine) sugar

55 ml / 2 fl. oz / ¼ cup cold water

Method

Grease and line a baking tray with greaseproof paper.

Mix together the water and sugar in a saucepan for the garnish. Cook over a moderate heat, swirling gently, until you have a dark caramel.

Pour the caramel onto the tray and sprinkle the hazelnut on top before leaving to set to one side.

Preheat the oven to 180°C (160° fan) / 350F / gas 4.

Roll the pastry out on a lightly floured surface to ½ cm thickness. Cut out 4 rounds of pastry and use to line 4 individual 4 inch fluted tartlet cases. Prick the bases with a fork and trim any excess pastry.

Line with greaseproof paper and fill with baking beans before blind-baking for 12-15 minutes until golden at the edges.

Remove from the oven and discard the greaseproof paper and baking beans.

Return to the oven for 3-4 minutes to brown the base before removing to a wire rack.

Melt the chocolate, butter and cream in a heatproof bowl set atop a saucepan of simmering water, stirring occasionally. Move to one side to allow the chocolate to cool and thicken.

Pour into the pastry tartlets and garnish with hazelnut brittle.

Makes: 4   Preparation time: **10-15 minutes**   Cooking time: **15-20 minutes**

Pork, Brie and Pepper Crostini

Ingredients

½ flute baguette, cut into 8 slices

30 ml / 1 fl. oz / 2 tbsp sunflower oil

225 g / 8 oz / 1 ½ cups pork fillet

1 large green pepper, deseeded and cut into 8 squares

110 g / 4 oz / 1 cup Brie, cut into 8 even slices

salt and pepper

a few sprigs of rosemary, chopped

Method

Preheat the oven to 190°C (170° fan) / 375F / gas 5.

Preheat the grill to hot and arrange the pepper on a grilling tray.

Season and grill for 2-3 minutes until starting to soften and colour.

Remove to one side to cool.

Heat a large frying pan over a moderate heat until hot.

Cut the pork fillet into 8 even slices and rub with the oil.

Season well before searing until golden all over.

Transfer to the oven for 6-8 minutes until the pork is firm yet slightly springy to the touch.

Remove from the oven and leave to rest on a warm plate for 5 minutes.

Place a slice of pepper on top of the baguette slices and follow with the pork then Brie.

Grill for 1-2 minutes until the cheese starts to melt.

Remove and garnish with rosemary before serving.

Serves: **4**   Preparation time: **10 minutes**   Cooking time: **15 minutes**

Lemon Curd Tartlets

Ingredients

250 g / 9 oz ready-made shortcrust pastry

a little plain (all purpose) flour, for dusting

110 g / 4 oz / ½ cup caster (superfine) sugar

100 g / 3 ½ oz / ½ cup unsalted butter, cubed

30 g / 1 oz / 2 tbsp cornflour (cornstarch)

125 ml / 4 ½ fl. oz / ½ cup freshly squeezed lemon juice

75 ml / 3 fl. oz / ⅓ cup cold water

3 medium egg yolks

1 medium egg

50 g / 2 oz / ⅓ cup good-quality dark chocolate, chopped

Method

Preheat the oven to 180°C (160° fan) / 350F / gas 4.

Roll the pastry out on a lightly floured surface to ½ cm thickness.

Cut out 4 rounds of pastry and use to line 4 individual 4 inch fluted tartlet cases.

Prick the bases with a fork and trim any excess pastry.

Line with greaseproof paper and fill with baking beans before blind-baking for 12-15 minutes until golden at the edges.

Remove from the oven and discard the greaseproof paper and baking beans.

Return to the oven for 3 minutes to brown then cool on a wire rack.

Combine the cornflour and sugar in a saucepan, then add the lemon juice and water

Cook over a medium heat, stirring constantly until thickened.

Once the mixture starts to bubble, remove from the heat and beat in the butter.

Combine the egg yolks and whole egg and beat into the mixture.

Return to the heat and stir until the mix drops from a spoon with a light tap.

Melt the chocolate in a heatproof bowl set atop a small saucepan of simmering wate

Spoon the lemon curd into the cases and drizzle with melted chocolate.

Makes: **4**   Preparation time: **10-15 minutes**   Cooking time: **20-25 minutes**

Rolled Ham Appetizers

Ingredients

1 sheet of ready-made puff pastry

a little plain (all purpose) flour, for dusting

1 tbsp olive oil

8 slices of prosciutto ham

a few sprigs of rosemary

Method

Preheat the oven to 200°C (180° fan) / 400F / gas 6.

Grease and line a large baking tray with greaseproof paper.

Roll the pastry out on a lightly floured surface to ½ cm thickness.

Brush with olive oil and cover with the slices of prosciutto ham.

Roll into a log and use a sharp knife to cut ½ inch slices.

Arrange flat on the baking tray and bake for 10-12 minutes until the pastry has puffed and is golden in colour.

Remove from the oven and leave to cool a little before garnishing with rosemary and serving.

Makes: **6**   Preparation time: **5-10 minutes**   Cooking time: **10 minutes**

Walnut and Pear Mini Chocolate and Vanilla Cakes

Ingredients

110 g / 4 oz / ½ cup golden caster (superfine) sugar

110 g / 4 oz / ½ cup margarine

110 g / 4 oz / ⅔ cup self-raising flour

50 g / 2 oz / ½ cup walnut halves, finely chopped

1 tbsp unsalted butter, softened

1 tbsp walnut flour

2 large eggs

2 ripe pears, peeled, cored and finely diced

30 g / 1 oz / 2 tbsp caster (superfine) sugar

Method

Preheat the oven to 180°C (160° fan) / 350F / gas 4.

Grease a 12-hole decorative cupcake tin with the unsalted butter.

Combine the sugar, margarine, self-raising flour, walnut flour and eggs in a large mixing bowl.

Beat for 2-3 minutes until smooth and creamy.

Fold through the pear and walnut halves before spooning into the cupcake tin.

Bake for 15-20 minutes; test with a wooden toothpick, if it comes out clean, they are done.

Remove to a wire rack to cool for 5 minutes before turning out and dusting their tops with caster sugar.

Serve warm or cold.

Makes: **12**   Preparation time: **10-15 minutes**   Cooking time: **10-15 minutes**

Mini Tofu Brochettes

Ingredients

30 ml / 1 fl. oz / 2 tbsp olive oil

110 g / 4 oz / 1 cup pressed tofu, cut into 8 even cubes

8 cherry tomatoes

8 dried apricot halves

1 green pepper, deseeded

salt and pepper

1 tbsp mini wholewheat cracker sticks

Method

Cut the pepper into 8 even squares and set to one side.

Heat a large frying pan over a moderate heat until hot.

Coat the cubes of tofu in oil and season generously before pan-frying for 3-4 minutes until golden-brown in colour all over.

Remove to kitchen paper to drain.

Add the peppers and apricot halves to the pan and fry for 1 minute, tossing occasionally.

Thread the cherry tomatoes, apricot halves and green pepper onto the cubes of tofu before serving with the crackers.

Serves: **4**   Preparation time: **10 minutes**   Cooking time: **10 minutes**

Apple, Pecan and Maple Cakes

Ingredients

110 g / 4 oz / ⅔ cup self-raising flour

110 g / 4 oz / ½ cup margarine

75 g / 3 oz / ¾ cup pecan halves

55 g / 2 oz / ¼ cup caster (superfine) sugar

55 g / 2 oz / ¼ cup maple syrup

1 tbsp cornflour (cornstarch)

1 large eating apple, peeled, cored and finely diced

2 large eggs

a pinch of salt

1 tbsp icing (confectioners') sugar

Method

Preheat the oven to 180°C (160° fan) / 350F / gas 4.

Line a 12-hole rectangular cupcake tray with 8 cases.

Combine the flour, cornflour, sugar, maple syrup, margarine, eggs and salt in a large mixing bowl.

Beat for 2-3 minutes until smooth and creamy.

Fold through the apple and most of the pecans.

Spoon into the cases and dot the tops with the remaining pecans.

Bake for 20-25 minutes; test with a wooden toothpick, if it comes out clean, the cakes are done.

Remove to a wire rack and leave to cool before peeling off their cases.

Dust with icing sugar before serving.

Makes: **8**   Preparation time: **10 minutes**   Cooking time: **10 minutes**

Feta and Potato Turnovers

Ingredients

250 g / 9 oz ready-made puff pastry

a little plain (all purpose) flour, for dusting

30 ml / 1 fl. oz / 2 tbsp olive oil

450 g / 1 lb / 3 cups white potatoes, peeled and diced

100 g / 3 ½ oz / 1 cup feta, diced

1 medium egg, beaten

2 tsp caraway seeds

a small handful of picked flat-leaf parsley leaves, finely chopped

salt and pepper

Method

Cook the potato in a saucepan of boiling water until tender; 15-20 minutes.

Drain and leave to cool a little before running under cold water.

Once cool enough to handle, dry on kitchen paper before chopping and adding to the feta, olive oil and seasoning in a mixing bowl.

Preheat the oven to 180°C (160° fan) / 350F / gas 4.

Line a large baking tray with greaseproof paper.

Roll the pastry out on a lightly floured surface to ½ cm thickness.

Cut out 4 7 inch rounds of pastry and arrange the potato and feta mixture in the middle of the rounds.

Top with a sprinkle of chopped parsley before wetting the rim of the pastry with a little water using your fingertip.

Fold the bottom end over the filling and seal well with the opposite end.

Transfer to the baking tray and brush with the beaten egg.

Sprinkle half a teaspoon of caraway seeds on top of each turnover and bake for 18-22 minutes until the pastry is golden and cooked.

Remove from the oven and leave to cool a little before serving.

Makes: **4**   Preparation time: **10-15 minutes**   Cooking time: **20-25 minutes**

Party

Mini Chocolate and Vanilla Cakes

Ingredients

For the dark chocolate sponge:

150 g / 5 oz / 1 cup plain (all purpose) flour

125 ml / 4 ½ fl. oz / ½ cup vegetable oil

125 ml / 4 ½ fl. oz / ½ cup cold water

125 g / 4 ½ oz / ½ cup sour cream

110 g / 4 oz / ½ cup caster (superfine) sugar

50 g / 2 oz / ⅓ cup good-quality cocoa powder

1 tbsp distilled white vinegar, 1 large egg

1 tsp baking powder, a pinch of salt

For the buttercreams:

450 g / 1 lb / 2 cups unsalted butter, softened

375 g / 13 oz / 3 cups icing sugar

30 g / 1 oz / 2 tbsp good-quality cocoa powder

30 ml / 1 fl. oz / 2 tbsp whole milk

1 tbsp vanilla extract

1 tbsp good-quality cocoa powder

Method

Preheat the oven to 180°C (160° fan) / 350F / gas 4.

Grease and line a 13 inch x 9 inch x 1 inch jelly roll pan with greaseproof paper.

Sift the flour, cocoa powder, baking powder, sugar and salt into a mixing bowl.

Whisk in the oil and sour cream, mixing well to incorporate, then whisk in the water in a slow, steady stream.

Add the vinegar and egg, whisking again before pouring into the jelly roll pan.

Bake for 18-22 minutes. Remove to a wire rack to cool.

Pulse together the butter and icing sugar in a food processor until smooth.

Spoon one third of the buttercream into a bowl, beating the vanilla extract into it.

Add the cocoa powder and milk to the food processor and pulse to combine.

Cut the sponge in half and spread the chocolate buttercream on one half.

Sit the other sponge on top, then spread the vanilla buttercream on top.

Run the tines of a fork across and lightly dust with cocoa powder. Cut into squares before serving.

Makes: **16**   Preparation time: **10-15 minutes**   Cooking time: **20-25 minutes**

Baked Risotto Balls

Ingredients

175 g / 6 oz / 1 ½ cups golden breadcrumbs

100 g / 3 ½ oz / ½ cup arborio rice

30 ml / 1 fl. oz / 2 tbsp olive oil

1 tbsp butter

1 shallot, finely chopped

1 clove of garlic, minced

½ red onion, finely chopped

55 ml / 2 fl. oz / ¼ cup dry white wine

500 ml / 18 fl. oz / 2 cups vegetable stock, kept hot on the stove

a small handful of flat-leaf parsley, finely chopped

salt and pepper

a small handful of rocket (arugula) leaves

a small handful of flat-leaf parsley, leaves picked

Method

Heat together the oil and butter in a saucepan set over a medium heat.

Sauté the shallots gently for 4-5 minutes then add the garlic and continue to cook for a further 2 minutes.

Add the rice and coat thoroughly in the butter, oil and shallot mixture and cook until the grains start to turn translucent.

Add the white wine and increase the heat to allow it to evaporate away.

Add one ladle of stock to the risotto, stirring constantly.

Continue adding one ladle of stock until the rice is soft; usually 30 minutes.

Stir through the parsley, adjust the seasoning to taste and spoon into a bowl before covering and chilling for 2 hours.

Preheat the oven to 190°C (170° fan) / 375F / gas 5.

Roll tablespoons of the cooked risotto into balls then coat in the breadcrumbs.

Arrange on a greaseproof paper-lined baking tray and top with a little red onion.

Bake for 10-12 minutes until warmed through.

Serve on platters sat atop parsley leaves and garnished with rocket leaves.

Serves: 4   Preparation time: **15 minutes**   Cooking time: **45-55 minutes**

Chocolate, Walnut and Orange Cookies

Ingredients

110 g / 4 oz / ⅔ cup plain (all purpose) flour

110 g / 4 oz / ½ cup margarine, softened

110 g / 4 oz / ½ cup caster (superfine) sugar

85 g / 3 ½ oz / ½ cup dark brown soft sugar

50 g / 2 oz / ½ cup walnut halved, chopped

40 g / 1 ½ oz / ¼ cup good-quality cocoa powder

30 g / 1 oz / 2 tbsp preserved stem ginger, drained and chopped

1 medium egg

1 tsp vanilla extract

1 tsp bicarbonate of (baking) soda

1 tsp salt

18 pieces of candied orange peel

Method

Preheat the oven to 180°C (160° fan) / 350F / gas 4.

Grease and line 2 baking trays with greaseproof paper.

Beat together the margarine and sugars until light and fluffy.

Beat in the egg and vanilla extract before sifting in the flour, cocoa powder, bicarbonate of soda and salt, mixing again.

Stir in the chopped walnuts and chopped stem ginger.

Take tablespoons of the dough and roll into balls before arranging on the baking trays, spaced apart.

Flatten a little and stud each with a piece of candied orange peel before baking for 12-15 minutes until set and starting to crack on top.

Remove to a wire rack to cool before serving.

Makes: **18**   Preparation time: **15 minutes**   Cooking time: **15 minutes**

Chicken Spring Rolls

Ingredients

30 ml / 1 fl. oz / 2 tbsp groundnut oil

8 spring roll wrappers

4 skinless chicken breasts, cut into thin strips

2 large onions, finely chopped

2 cloves of garlic, minced

2 large carrots, peeled and diced

4 spring onions (scallions), sliced

1 medium egg, beaten

1 tbsp rice wine vinegar

1 tbsp dark soy sauce

1 gem lettuce, leaves separated

a large sprig of mint leaves

55 ml / 2 fl. oz / ¼ cup plum sauce

Method

Preheat the oven to 200°C (180°C fan) / 400°F / gas 6.

Heat the groundnut oil in a large sauté pan set over a medium heat until hot

Sweat the onion, garlic and carrot until the onion turns translucent; 8-10 minutes, stirring frequently.

Add the chicken and spring onion, stir well, and continue cooking for 3 minutes before adding the soy sauce and rice wine vinegar.

Brush the rims of the wrappers with the beaten egg.

Spoon the chicken and vegetable filling into the middle of the wrappers and fold the ends in and over the filling.

Roll up tightly into cylinders and arrange on a baking tray.

Bake for 15-20 minutes until golden and crisp.

Remove from the oven and serve on top of lettuce leaves with plum sauce on the side and a garnish of mint leaves.

Serves: 4   Preparation time: **10-15 minutes**   Cooking time: **10-15 minutes**

Chocolate Brownies

Ingredients

175 g / 6 oz / 1 ¼ cups good-quality dark chocolate, chopped

110 g / 4 oz / ½ cup unsalted butter

110 g / 4 oz / ½ cup caster (superfine) sugar

110 g / 4 oz / ⅔ cup plain (all purpose) flour

100 g / 3 ½ oz / 1 cup walnut halves, finely chopped

100 g / 3 ½ oz / 1 cup pine nuts, finely chopped

30 g / 1 oz / 2 tbsp demerara sugar

3 large eggs

1 tsp baking powder

a pinch of salt

Method

Preheat the oven to 160°C (140° fan) / 325F / gas 3.

Grease and line a 7 inch square cake tin with greaseproof paper.

Melt the chocolate and butter together in a saucepan over a medium-low heat, stirring occasionally until smooth.

Remove from the heat and allow to cool.

In a large mixing bowl, whisk the eggs until thick then add the sugar and continue to whisk until glossy.

Beat in the melted chocolate mixture, then fold in the flour and baking powder until incorporated.

Fold through half of the pine nuts and pour into the tin.

Top with the remaining pine nuts, walnuts and demerara sugar.

Bake for 30-35 minutes; test with a wooden toothpick, if it comes out almost clean, the brownies are done.

Remove from the oven and leave to cool before turning out and cutting into squares.

Serves: **8**   Preparation time: **10-15 minutes**   Cooking time: **10-15 minutes**

Crispy Chicken Bites

Ingredients

For the chicken bites:
1 l / 1 pint 16 fl. oz / 4 cups groundnut oil, for deep-frying

4 skinless chicken breasts, sliced into strips

2 large eggs, beaten

50 g / 2 oz / ⅓ cup plain (all purpose) flour

110 g / 4 oz / 1 cup panko breadcrumbs

110 g / 4 oz / 4 cups cornflakes, crushed

salt and pepper

For the sauce:
125 g / 4 ½ oz / ½ cup plain yoghurt

1 tbsp mayonnaise

a few chive stalks, finely chopped

salt and pepper

Method

Heat the groundnut oil in a large, heavy-based saucepan until hot; you can tell when the oil is hot enough as bubbles appear on a wooden spoon dipped in the hot oil.

Whisk together the yoghurt, mayonnaise and seasoning in a small bowl until smooth.

Cover and chill until ready to serve.

Mix together the breadcrumbs and cornflakes in a shallow dish.

Dry the chicken pieces and season well.

Coat in the flour, shaking off any excess, before dipping in the egg and coating in breadcrumb mixture.

Arrange on a lined baking tray until you have coated all the chicken.

Deep-fry the battered chicken in batches until golden-brown in colour; 3-4 minutes usually.

Remove with a slotted spoon to kitchen paper to drain.

Spoon the sauce into serving pots and garnish with chive.

Serve alongside the chicken bites.

Serves: **4**   Preparation time: **10 minutes**   Cooking time: **15-20 minutes**

Peach and Raspberry Shortbread Tartlets

Ingredients

225 g / 8 oz / 1 ½ cups plain (all purpose) flour

a little extra plain (all purpose) flour, for dusting

55 g / 2 oz / ⅓ cup cornflour (cornstarch)

225 g / 8 oz / 1 cup unsalted butter, cubed

110 g / 4 oz / 1 cup ground almonds

75 g / 3 oz / ⅔ cup icing (confectioners') sugar

½ tsp salt

125 g / 4 ½ oz / ½ cup plain yoghurt

12 raspberries

2 white peaches, de-stoned and cut into eighths

1 tbsp shelled pistachios, finely chopped

1 tbsp pink sugar crystals

Method

Pulse together the flour, cornflour, ground almonds, salt, icing sugar and butter in a food processor until a dough comes together.

Gently knead the dough on a lightly floured work surface before wrapping in clingfilm and chilling for 60 minutes.

Preheat the oven to 170°C (150°C fan) / 325F / gas 3.

Grease and line a large baking tray with greaseproof paper.

Remove the dough from the fridge and roll out on a lightly floured work surface to ½ inch thickness.

Use a 4 inch straight-sided cookie cutter to stamp out 6 rounds of dough before lifting carefully onto the baking tray.

Bake for 20-25 minutes until the shortbread starts to colour on top.

Remove to a wire rack to cool.

Once cool, top with a tablespoon of yoghurt, a couple of slices of peach and two raspberries before garnishing with chopped pistachios and sugar crystals.

Makes: **6**   Preparation time: **10-15 minutes**   Cooking time: **15-20 minutes**

Stuffed Courgette Rolls

Ingredients

55 ml / 2 fl. oz / ¼ cup olive oil

1 large courgette (zucchini), sliced on a mandolin into ½ cm slices

1 large onion, sliced

1 clove of garlic, minced

75 g / 3 oz / ½ cup pitted Kalamata olives, chopped

4 large vine tomatoes, blanched

salt and pepper

a few sprigs of rosemary

a few sprigs of thyme

Method

Preheat the oven to 190°C (170° fan) / 375F / gas 5.

Grease and line a baking tray with greaseproof paper.

Heat the olive oil in a sauté pan set over a medium heat.

Sweat the onion and garlic with a little seasoning for 6-7 minutes until the onions are soft and translucent.

Deseed and dice the tomatoes before adding to the onion along with the olive

Adjust the seasoning to taste and set to one side.

Lay the slices of courgette flat on the baking tray and spoon tablespoons of th onion, tomato and olive mixture onto them before rolling tightly.

Secure using toothpicks and season the outsides before baking for 8-10 minu

Remove from the oven and remove the toothpicks.

Arrange upright on a serving plate garnished with rosemary and thyme.

Serve immediately.

Serves: **4**   Preparation time: **10-15 minutes**   Cooking time: **20-25 minutes**

Bilberry Tartlet

Ingredients

200 g / 7 oz ready-made sweet shortcrust pastry

a little plain (all purpose) flour, for dusting

200 g / 7 oz / 2 cups bilberries (use blueberries if not available)

125 ml / 4 ½ fl. oz / ½ cup whipping cream

1 tbsp icing (confectioners') sugar

1 tbsp lemon juice

½ tsp vanilla extract

1 lime, finely zested

Method

Preheat the oven to 180°C (160° fan) / 350F / gas 4.

Roll the pastry out on a lightly floured surface to ½ cm thickness.

Cut out 4 rounds of pastry and use to line 4 individual 4 inch fluted tartlet cases.

Prick the bases with a fork and trim any excess, overhanging pastry.

Line with greaseproof paper and fill with baking beans before blind-baking for 12-15 minutes until golden at the edges.

Remove from the oven and discard the greaseproof paper and baking beans.

Return to the oven for 3-4 minutes to brown the base before removing to a wire rack to cool.

Toss the bilberries with the icing sugar and lemon juice in a mixing bowl.

Whip the cream with the vanilla extract until soft peaks form.

Spoon the cream into the tartlet cases and top with bilberries, making sure they evenly cover the cream.

Garnish with lime zest before serving.

Makes: 4   Preparation time: **10 minutes**   Cooking time: **15 minutes**

Mushroom and Ham Mini Tartlets

Ingredients

24 ready-made mini tartlet cases

55 ml / 2 fl. oz / ¼ cup olive oil

1 tbsp butter

300 g / 10 ½ oz / 4 cups button mushrooms, finely chopped

150 g / 5 oz / 1 cup Serrano ham, sliced

2 celery stalks, finely diced

1 onion, finely chopped

a small bunch of flat-leaf parsley, finely chopped

salt and pepper

a few sprigs of chervil leaves

Method

Heat half of the olive oil in a large frying pan set over a medium heat until hot

Sweat the onion and celery with a little seasoning until soft and translucent; 5-6 minutes.

Add the ham and continue to cook, stirring occasionally, for 3-4 minutes.

Remove the contents of the pan to a plate and wipe the pan clean.

Add the remaining oil and the butter and heat until the butter has melted.

Add the mushrooms and sauté with some seasoning for 7-8 minutes, tossing occasionally, until they start to colour.

Add the onion and ham mixture back to the pan along with the chopped parsley

Adjust the seasoning to taste if necessary before spooning into the tartlet cases

Serve warm or cold with sprig of chervil as a garnish.

Makes: **24**   Preparation time: **20 minutes**   Cooking time: **10 minutes**

Chocolate and Hazelnut Lollipops

Ingredients

300 g / 10 ½ oz / 2 cups good-quality dark chocolate, roughly chopped

250 ml / 9 fl. oz / 1 cup whipping cream

100 g / 3 ½ oz / 1 cup blanched whole hazelnuts (cob nuts)

50 g / 2 oz / ¼ cup unsalted butter

12 Mikado, tops trimmed

sunflower oil, for shaping

Method

Place the chocolate in a large heatproof mixing bowl.

Combine the cream and butter in a saucepan and heat over a moderate heat until simmering.

Once the butter has fully melted and the mixture is simmering, remove from the heat and pour over the chocolate.

Whisk until you have a smooth mixture.

Cover the bowl and chill for 4 hours.

Meanwhile, pulse the hazelnuts in a food processor until they are finely crushed before tipping into a shallow dish.

To make the truffles, use a melon baller to take out scoops of the truffle mixture.

Using lightly oiled hands, roll into marshmallow shapes, then roll in the crushed hazelnuts until evenly coated.

Skewer them carefully with the Mikado before serving.

Makes: **12**   Preparation time: **10 minutes**   Cooking time: **15 minutes**

Stuffed Cherry Tomatoes

Ingredients

8 vine cherry tomatoes, tops removed and deseeded

110 g / 4 oz / ½ cup cream cheese

4 pimento-stuffed green olives, sliced

a few chive stalks, finely chopped

a few chive stalks

Method

Beat the cream cheese in a mixing bowl until smooth and creamy.

Spoon into a piping bag fitted with a small star-shaped nozzle.

Pipe into the cherry tomatoes before sprinkling with chopped chives.

Sit slices of olive on top of the cream cheese and arrange on a serving plate

Garnish with a chive stalks before serving.

Serves: 4   Preparation time: **10-15 minutes**

Chocolate and Pistachio Bites

Ingredients

175 g / 6 oz / ¾ cup unsalted butter, cubed

110 g / 4 oz / ⅔ cup gingernut biscuits (use digestive biscuits if not available), chopped

110 g / 4 oz / 1 cup shelled pistachios

100 g / 3 ½ oz / ⅔ cup good-quality dark chocolate, chopped

75 g / 2 oz / ⅓ cup good-quality cocoa powder

1 tbsp shelled pistachios, chopped

4-6 speculos biscuits (use malted milk biscuits if not available)

Method

Melt the chocolate and butter in a heatproof bowl set atop a saucepan of simmering water, stirring occasionally.

Once melted, remove from the heat and leave to cool a little before stirring in the gingernut biscuits, cocoa powder and pistachios.

Once the mixture starts to cool and thicken, spoon onto a sheet of greaseproof paper and roll into a sausage shape.

Tie the ends and chill for 3-4 hours until set.

Unroll the sausage and cut into slices using a warm, wet knife.

Serve with the speculos biscuits and chopped pistachios sprinkled on top.

Serves: **4**   Preparation time: **10-15 minutes**   Cooking time: **10 minutes**

Garlic and Herb Cookie Sandwiches

Ingredients

For the cookies:

225 g / 8 oz / 1 ⅓ cup plain (all purpose) flour, sifted

a little extra plain (all purpose) flour, for dusting

110 g / 4 oz / 1 cup Parmesan cheese, grated

110 g / 4 oz / ½ cup unsalted butter, melted

2 medium egg yolk

2 tsp dried basil, 2 tsp dried oregano

½ tsp garlic powder, ½ tsp salt

For the filling:

300 g / 10 ½ oz / 3 cup goats' cheese

a small bunch of chive stalks, finely chopped

1 tbsp double (heavy) cream

salt and pepper

Method

Mix the flour, butter, Parmesan, garlic powder and salt in a food processor.

Pulse until the mixture resembles fine breadcrumbs.

Add the egg yolk and pulse again until a dough form; add a little warm water if dough is too dry or doesn't come together easily.

Turn the mixture out onto a work surface and form into a ball, wrap in clingfilm chill for 15 minutes.

Preheat the oven to 180°C (160°C) / 350F / gas 4.

Grease and line 2 baking trays with greaseproof paper.

Roll the dough to ½ cm thickness on a lightly floured surface.

Using a 4 cm straight-sided cookie cutter, cut out 16 rounds and place on baking

Sprinkle the dried herbs on top of the rounds and press in lightly before baking 10-12 minutes. Remove to a wire rack to cool.

Pulse together the chives, goats' cheese, cream and chives.

Spread on the underside of 8 of the cookies before sandwiching together with t other 8 cookies and serving.

Makes: **8**   Preparation time: **10 minutes**   Cooking time: **15-20 minutes**

Mini Lemon Meringue Pies

Ingredients

250 g / 9 oz ready-made shortcrust pastry

a little plain (all purpose) flour, for dusting

110 g / 4 oz / ½ cup caster (superfine) sugar

100 g / 3 ½ oz / ½ cup unsalted butter, cubed

30 g / 1 oz / 2 tbsp cornflour (cornstarch)

125 ml / 4 ½ fl. oz / ½ cup freshly squeezed lemon juice

75 ml / 3 fl. oz / ⅓ cup cold water

3 medium egg yolks

1 medium egg

1 large egg white

55 g / 2 oz / ¼ cup caster (superfine) sugar

a pinch of cream of tartar

a pinch of salt

Method

Preheat the oven to 130°C (110° fan) / 250F / gas ½. Grease and line a baking tray with greaseproof paper. Whisk the egg white with a pinch of salt until soft peaks form.

Add the cream of tartar and the sugar, one spoon at a time, beating well until thick and glossy. Spoon into a piping bag and pipe onto the tray in swirled finger shapes.

Bake for 1 hour, then turn the oven off and leave to cool with the door ajar. Remove once cool and heat the oven to 180°C (160° fan) / 350F / gas 4.

Roll the pastry out on a floured surface to ½ cm thickness. Cut out 4 rectangles of pastry and use to line 4 tartlet cases. Prick the bases with a fork and trim excess pastry.

Line with greaseproof paper and fill with baking beans, then blind-bake for 12-15 minutes.

Remove from the oven and discard the greaseproof paper and baking beans.

Return to the oven for 3 minutes to brown the base before removing to a wire rack to cool.

Combine the cornflour and sugar in a saucepan, then add the lemon juice and water.

Cook over a medium heat, stirring constantly until thickened. Once the mixture starts to bubble, remove from the heat and beat in the butter.

Combine the egg yolks and whole egg and beat into the mixture.

Return to the heat and stir constantly for a few minutes until the mixture drops from a spoon with a light tap. Spoon into the tartlet cases and top with a meringue finger.

Makes: 4   Preparation time: **10 minutes**   Cooking time: **25-30 minutes**

Chilli and Aniseed Tofu Appetizers

Ingredients

55 ml / 2 fl. oz / ¼ cup sunflower oil

225 g / 8 oz / 2 cups pressed tofu, cubed

1 tsp ground star anise

½ tsp chilli (chili) powder

salt and pepper

½ tsp chilli (chili) powder

a small handful of beansprouts

Method

Coat the tofu in the oil and sprinkle over the chilli powder, ground star anise and seasoning, tossing well.

Heat a large frying pan over a moderate heat until hot and pan-fry the tofu until golden-brown in colour all over.

Drain on kitchen paper before arranging on serving plates and garnishing with a dusting of chilli powder and some beansprouts.

Serves: **4**   Preparation time: **10 minutes**   Cooking time: **10 minutes**

Lime Madeleines

Ingredients

125 g / 4 ½ oz / 1 cup icing (confectioners') sugar, sifted

115 g / 4 oz / ½ cup unsalted butter, melted and cooled

100 g / 3 ½ oz / ⅔ cup plain (all purpose) flour, sifted

1 lime, juiced and finely zested

½ tsp baking powder

a pinch of salt

1 lime

a small sprig of bay leaves

Method

Preheat the oven to 180°C (160° fan) / 350F / gas 4.

Grease a 12-hole madeleine tray.

Beat together the eggs, icing sugar, salt and vanilla extract in a large mixing bowl until thick and shiny.

Fold in the flour, 25 g at a time, as well as the baking powder.

Once all the flour has been added, fold in the melted butter until incorporated then fold in the lime juice and zest.

Spoon into the moulds, leaving them about three-quarters full with the batter.

Bake for 12-14 minutes until golden and risen.

Remove and allow them to cool in the tray for a few minutes before turning out onto a wire rack to cool.

Slice half of the lime and serve alongside the madeleines with the remaining lime half and a sprig of bay leaves.

Makes: **12**   Preparation time: **10 minutes**   Cooking time: **10 minutes**

Sun-dried Tomato & Goats' Cheese Balls

Ingredients

200 g / 7 oz / 2 cups goats' cheese

75 g / 3 oz / ½ cup sun-dried tomatoes, sliced

a small bunch of chive stalks, finely chopped

freshly ground black pepper

a few sprigs of coriander (cilantro), finely chopped

a few basil leaves, sliced

Method

Divide the goats' cheese into 8 and roll into balls between lightly oiled palms

Stud with slices of Sun-dried tomato before rolling in pepper and chives.

Chill until ready to serve.

Garnish with coriander and basil leaves.

Serves: 4   Preparation time: **10 minutes**   Cooking time: **5-10 minutes**

Chocolate and Coconut Tiger Cookies

Ingredients

225 g / 8 oz / 3 cups desiccated coconut

200 g / 7 oz / 1 ⅓ cup good-quality dark chocolate, chopped

110 g / 4 oz / ½ cup caster (superfine) sugar

30 g / 1 oz / 2 tbsp ground almonds

2 large egg whites

¼ tsp cream of tartar

a pinch of salt

Method

Preheat the oven to 160°C (140° fan) / 325F / gas 3.

Grease and line a large baking tray with greaseproof paper.

Whisk the egg whites in a large, clean bowl until frothy, then add the cream of tartar and continue whisking until soft peaks form.

Add the sugar a tablespoon at a time as you continue whisking, until you have stiff glossy peaks.

Add the ground almonds, salt and coconut, folding gently to mix well.

Spoon into a piping bag fitted with a straight-sided nozzle.

Pipe fingers of the mixture onto the baking tray, spaced apart, before baking for 22-25 minutes until golden-brown in colour.

Remove to a wire rack to cool.

Melt the chocolate in a heatproof bowl set atop a saucepan of simmering water, stirring occasionally.

Once melted, take tablespoons of the melted chocolate and drizzle back and forth over the cookies. Leave the chocolate to set before serving.

Makes: **12**   Preparation time: **10 minutes**   Cooking time: **15-20 minutes**

Exquisite

Chocolate Truffles

Ingredients

300 g / 10 ½ oz / 2 cups good-quality dark chocolate, chopped

300 ml / 10 ½ fl. oz / 1 ⅕ cups double (heavy) cream

55 g / 2 oz / ¼ cup unsalted butter

55 g / 2 oz / ⅓ cup cocoa powder

a little sunflower oil

Method

Place the chocolate in a large heatproof mixing bowl.

Place the cream and butter in a saucepan and bring to a simmer over a moderate heat.

Once the butter has fully melted and the mixture is simmering, remove from the heat and pour over the chocolate.

Beat until you have a smooth mixture, then cover the bowl and chill for 4 hours.

To make the truffles, remove the chocolate mixture from the fridge and let sit at room temperature for 10 minutes.

Use a melon baller to take out scoops of the truffle mixture.

Using lightly oiled hands, roll into truffle shapes then roll in the cocoa powder to lightly coat.

Shake off any excess before serving in a bowl.

Makes: **24**   Preparation time: **5-10 minutes**   Cooking time: **10-15 minutes**

Smoked Salmon and Seaweed Rolls

Ingredients

150 g / 5 oz / 1 cup smoked salmon slices

30 g / 1 oz / ½ cup crispy seaweed

4 chive stalks

a few extra chive stalks

Method

Blanch the chive stalks in a saucepan of boiling water for 10 seconds.

Remove and refresh in iced water.

Crush the seaweed until finely ground and set to one side.

Lay the salmon on a flat surface covered with clingfilm and sprinkle the seaweed on top.

Roll up tightly and use a blanched chive stalks to tie the rolls.

Serve upright on plates garnished with chive stalks.

Serves: **4**   Preparation time: **5-10 minutes**   Cooking time: **5-10 minutes**

Strawberry and Rhubarb Tartlets

Ingredients

250 g / 9 oz ready shortcrust pastry

a little plain (all purpose) flour, for dusting

450 g / 1 lb / 4 cups rhubarb, diced

75 g / 3 oz / ⅓ cup caster (superfine) sugar

1 orange, juiced

4 strawberries, tops removed and thinly sliced

a few mint leaves, finely sliced

1 tbsp flaked (slivered) almonds, crushed

Method

Combine the rhubarb, sugar and orange juice in a saucepan.

Cook over a medium heat, stirring occasionally, until the rhubarb breaks down and is easily mashed with a fork.

Remove from the heat and mash until roughly puréed.

Preheat the oven to 180°C (160° fan) / 350F / gas 4.

Roll the pastry out on a lightly floured surface to ½ cm thickness.

Cut out 4 rounds of pastry and use to line 4 individual 4 inch tartlet cases.

Prick the bases with a fork and trim any excess, overhanging pastry.

Line with greaseproof paper and fill with baking beans before blind-baking for 12-15 minutes until golden at the edges.

Remove from the oven and discard the greaseproof paper and baking beans.

Return to the oven for 3-4 minutes to brown the base before removing to a wire rack to cool.

Once cool, fill with the rhubarb and top with strawberry slices.

Garnish with flaked almonds and mint before serving.

Makes: **4**   Preparation time: **10-15 minutes**   Cooking time: **20-25 minutes**

Polenta and Parma Ham Appetizers

Ingredients

375 g / 13 oz / 2 ½ cups
ready-made polenta

75 g / 3 oz / ½ cup sun-dried
tomatoes, drained

30 ml / 1 fl. oz / 2 tbsp olive oil

8 slices of Parma ham

½ courgette (zucchini), cut into 8 slices

salt and pepper

Method

Preheat the oven to 190°C (170° fan) / 375F / gas 5.

Grease and line a baking tray with greaseproof paper.

Use a 2 inch fluted cookie cutter to stamp out 8 rounds of polenta and arrange on the baking tray.

Drizzle with olive oil and season well before topping with a slice of courgette.

Bake for 8-10 minutes until the courgette is cooked and coloured on top.

Remove from the oven and top with a folded slice of ham and a piece of Sun-dried tomato, using a skewer to secure them on top of the polenta and courgette.

Serve immediately.

Serves: **4**   Preparation time: **10 minutes**   Cooking time: **10 minutes**

Raspberry and Cream Pastry Boats

Ingredients

4 sheets of ready-made filo pastry, kept under a damp cloth

55 g / 2 oz / ¼ cup unsalted butter, melted and cooled

250 ml / 9 fl. oz / 1 cup whole milk

55 g / 2 oz / ¼ cup caster (superfine) sugar

3 medium egg yolks

1 tsp vanilla extract

200 g / 7 oz / 2 cups raspberries

30 g / 1 oz / 2 tbsp shelled pistachios, finely chopped

a few flattened sprigs of mint

Method

Preheat the oven to 200°C (180° fan) / 400F / gas 6.

Grease and line a baking tray with greaseproof paper.

Brush each sheet of pastry with melted butter before sandwiching together one on top of another.

Cut into quarters and drape over 4 upturned, individual boat-shaped moulds.

Place on the baking tray and bake for 15-18 minutes until golden and crisp.

Meanwhile, mix the vanilla extract and milk in a saucepan and heat until boiling.

Remove to one side to cool.

Whisk the egg yolks and sugar in a bowl, then sift in the flour and cornflour, whisking again until smooth. Add the milk and vanilla, whisking all the time.

Pour back into the saucepan and cook for 2 minutes until thickened.

Transfer to a clean bowl and cover the surface with clingfilm before chilling.

Remove the pastry to a wire rack to cool.

Once cool, fill with the pastry cream and dot with raspberries.

Garnish with pistachios and mint leaves before serving.

Serves: 4   Preparation time: **10 minutes**   Cooking time: **15-20 minutes**

Beef Carpaccio and Tapenade Appetizers

Ingredients

150 g / 5 oz / 1 cup beef fillet, trimmed

150 g / 5 oz / 1 cup pitted black olives

55 ml / 2 fl. oz / ¼ cup extra-virgin olive oil

2 preserved anchovy fillet, drained and chopped

1 clove of garlic, chopped

½ lemon, juiced

8 large basil leaves

salt and pepper

25 g / 1 oz / ¼ cup Parmesan cheese, shaved

Method

Place the beef in the freezer for 10 minutes to firm up.

Finely slice the beef using a sharp chef's knife so that you have 8 even slices then chill as you prepare the tapenade.

Blitz together the anchovy, garlic, lemon juice, black olives and half of the olive oil in a food processor until smooth.

Adjust the seasoning to taste and loosen with more olive oil if needed.

Spoon a scant tablespoon of the tapenade onto the beef slices and roll to envelope.

Sit upright on basil leaves sat on ceramic soup spoons.

Garnish with shaved Parmesan cheese on top before serving.

Serves: **4**   Preparation time: **10 minutes**   Cooking time: **10-15 minutes**

Coconut and Rum Truffles

Ingredients

300 g / 10 ½ oz / 2 cups good-quality white chocolate, chopped

300 ml / 10 ½ fl. oz / 1 ⅕ cups double (heavy) cream

55 g / 2 oz / ¼ cup unsalted butter

55 ml / 2 fl. oz / ¼ cup white rum

225 g / 8 oz / 3 cups desiccated coconut

a little sunflower oil

Method

Place the chocolate in a large heatproof mixing bowl.

Place the cream, rum and butter in a saucepan and bring to a simmer over a moderate heat.

Once the butter has fully melted and the mixture is simmering, remove from the heat and pour over the chocolate.

Beat until you have a smooth mixture, then cover the bowl and chill for 4 hours.

To make the truffles, remove the chocolate mixture from the fridge and let sit at room temperature for 10 minutes.

Use a melon baller to take out scoops of the truffle mixture.

Using lightly oiled hands, roll into truffle shapes then roll in the desiccated coconut to coat.

Makes: **24**   Preparation time: **5-10 minutes**   Cooking time: **10-15 minutes**

Fried Manchego Appetizers

Ingredients

1 l / 1 pint 16 fl. oz / 3 cups groundnut oil, for deep-frying

300 g / 10 ½ oz / 3 cups Manchego cheese, cut into triangles

55 g / 2 oz / ⅓ cup plain (all purpose) flour

2 medium eggs, beaten

225 g / 8 oz / 2 cups panko breadcrumbs

salt and pepper

a few sprigs of dill

Method

Heat the groundnut oil in a large, heavy-based saucepan until hot; you can tell when the oil is hot enough as bubbles appear on a wooden spoon dipped in the hot oil.

Coat the cheese in the flour, shaking off any excess before dipping into the beaten egg.

Coat in the breadcrumbs and arrange on a lined baking tray.

Deep-fry in batches in the oil until golden-brown in colour all over; 2-3 minutes usually.

Remove with a slotted spoon to kitchen paper to drain.

Serve with sprigs of dill.

Serves: **4**   Preparation time: **10 minutes**   Cooking time: **15 minutes**

Cherry Cream Financier with Pistachio

Ingredients

110 g / 4 oz / ½ cup caster (superfine) sugar

110 g / 4 oz / ½ cup slightly salted butter, softened

1 tbsp unsalted butter, softened

110 g / 4 oz / 1 cup ground almonds

100 g / 3 ½ oz / ½ cup morello cherry jam

30 g / 1 oz / 2 tbsp plain (all purpose) flour, sifted

3 medium egg whites

a pinch of salt

110 g / 4 oz / ½ cup fromage blanc

50 g / 2 oz / ½ cup pistachios, finely chopped

8 cherries, stalks intact

Method

Brown the butter in a saucepan until nutty in aroma.

Strain through a fine sieve into a clean bowl, allowing it to cool.

Combine the flour, almonds and sugar in a mixing bowl.

Gently whisk the egg whites into this mixture and then fold through the cooled, melted butter and the cherry jam.

Chill for 30 minutes.

Preheat the oven to 180°C (160° fan) / 350F / gas 4.

Grease a 12-hole fluted bundt tin with unsalted butter.

Bake for 18-20 minutes until golden brown at the edges and risen.

Remove from the oven and cool on a wire rack.

Turn out once cool and top with a tablespoon of the fromage blanc and a cherry.

Sprinkle the pistachios over before serving.

Makes: **8**   Preparation time: **10 minutes**   Cooking time: **15 minutes**

Three Meats and Pepper Crostini

Ingredients

2 large slices of ciabatta

55 ml / 2 fl. oz / ¼ cup extra-virgin olive oil

150 g / 5 oz / 1 cup chistorra, cut into 8 bite-sized pieces

8 rashers of streaky bacon

8 slices of Serrano ham

2 red peppers, deseeded

a large handful of celery leaves

Method

Heat a griddle pan over a moderate heat until hot.

Preheat the grill to hot then cut the slices of ciabatta into 8 squares, and cut the red peppers into 8 similar sized pieces.

Brush the bread with olive oil and griddle until lightly coloured.

Remove from the pan and sit a slice of red pepper on top of each piece.

Grill until the pepper starts to soften and colour before removing and setting to one side.

Arrange the meats on a grilling tray and grill for 4-6 minutes, turning once until golden-brown in colour and crisp before removing.

Fold the bacon and ham in half and sit on top of the pepper, followed by celery leaves and chistorra, skewering them onto the bread using a skewer.

Serve immediately.

Serves: **4**   Preparation time: **10 minutes**   Cooking time: **10-15 minutes**

Pistachio Cookies with Strawberries

Ingredients

225 g / 8 oz / 1 ½ cups plain (all purpose) flour

a little extra plain (all purpose) flour, for dusting

55 g / 2 oz / ⅓ cup cornflour (cornstarch)

225 g / 8 oz / 1 cup unsalted butter, cubed

110 g / 4 oz / 1 cup shelled pistachios, finely chopped

75 g / 3 oz / ⅔ cup icing (confectioners') sugar

½ tsp salt

125 ml / 4 ½ fl. oz / ½ cup whipping cream

4 large strawberries, tops removed and quartered

1 tbsp shelled pistachios, finely chopped

Method

Pulse together the flour, cornflour, pistachios, salt, icing sugar and butter in a food processor until a dough comes together.

Gently knead the dough on a lightly floured work surface before wrapping in clingfilm and chilling for 60 minutes.

Preheat the oven to 170°C (150°C fan) / 325F / gas 3.

Grease and line a large baking tray with greaseproof paper.

Remove the dough from the fridge and roll out on a lightly floured work surface to 1 cm thickness.

Use a 3 inch fluted cookie cutter to stamp out 8 rounds of dough before lifting carefully onto the baking tray.

Bake for 18-20 minutes until the cookies start to colour on top.

Remove to a wire rack to cool.

Whip the cream until soft peaks form before serving with a couple of cookies and some quartered strawberries on top.

Garnish with chopped pistachios.

Makes: **8**   Preparation time: **10-15 minutes**   Cooking time: **15-20 minutes**

Bacon-Wrapped Prawns on Toast

Ingredients

2 slices of white sandwich bread, crusts removed

1 tbsp olive oil

8 raw prawns (shrimps), peeled with heads removed and tails intact

4 slices of streaky bacon, halved

4 chive stalks

salt and pepper

4 sprigs of flat-leaf parsley

1 tbsp extra-virgin olive oil

Method

Blanch the chive stalks in a saucepan of boiling water for 10 seconds before refreshing in iced water.

Drain and set to one side. Preheat the grill to hot.

Toast the bread until golden on both sides before removing and using a 2 inch cookie cutter to stamp 4 rounds out of the toast.

Wrap the perimeters of the toast rounds with the chive, trying to secure.

Wrap the prawns in half-slices of streaky bacon and thread two together using the skewers.

Arrange on a grilling tray and drizzle with olive oil and season well.

Grill for 4-5 minutes, turning once, until the bacon is crisp and the prawn is cooked.

Remove from the grill and skewer onto the toasts.

Arrange on serving plates, drizzle with a little extra-virgin olive oil and garnish with parsley.

Serves: **4**   Preparation time: **10-15 minutes**   Cooking time: **10 minutes**

Mini Summer Fruit Charlottes

Ingredients

20 savoiardi sponge fingers

350 ml / 12 fl. oz / 1 ⅓ cups whipping cream

65 g / 2 ½ oz / ½ cup icing (confectioners') sugar

1 tsp vanilla extract

100 g / 3 ½ oz / 1 cup raspberries

50 g / 2 oz / ½ cup blackcurrants

50 g / 2 oz / ½ cup blackberries

50 g / 2 oz / ½ cup redcurrants

1 tbsp icing (confectioners') sugar

Method

Whip the cream with the icing sugar and vanilla extract in a mixing bowl until soft peaks form.

Spoon into a piping bag fitted with a straight-sided nozzle.

Arrange 4 3 inch metal pastry rings on a greaseproof paper-lined baking tray.

Line the insides of each ring with 5 sponge fingers and pipe the cream into the centres so that it comes about three-quarters of the way up the insides of the fingers.

Layer the fruit on top and chill for at least 30 minutes.

Use a wide palette knife to lift the Charlottes onto serving plates.

Remove the pastry rings and tie the outsides of the Charlottes with decorative ribbon before dusting with icing sugar and serving.

Makes: **4**   Preparation time: **10 minutes**   Cooking time: **15 minutes**

Mushroom and Black Pudding Crostini

Ingredients

1 flute baguette, cut into 16 slices

1 l / 1 pint 16 fl. oz / 4 cups groundnut oil

16 button mushrooms

50 g / 2 oz / ⅓ cup plain (all purpose) flour

1 tsp dried rosemary

2 large eggs, beaten

225 g / 8 oz / 2 cups golden breadcrumbs

150 g / 5 oz / 1 cup black pudding,
cut into 16 slices

salt and pepper

For the onion rings
1 large onion, sliced into rings

75 g / 3 oz / ½ cup plain (all purpose) flour

1 tbsp cornflour (cornstarch)

plain (all purpose) flour, for dusting

125 ml / 4 ½ fl. oz / ½ cup sparkling water

Method

Heat the groundnut oil in a large, heavy-based saucepan until hot.

Mix the breadcrumbs with dried rosemary and seasoning in a shallow dish.

Dust the mushrooms with plain flour, shaking off any excess.

Dip in egg and coat in the breadcrumbs before arranging on a lined baking tray, then deep-fry in batches until golden-brown in colour all over; 2-3 minutes.

Remove with a slotted spoon to kitchen paper.

Mix the flour and cornflour for the onion rings in a mixing bowl.

Add the sparkling water and whisk briefly, adding some seasoning as you do.

Dip the onion rings in the batter and deep-fry for 1-2 minutes until golden and crisp.

Remove with a slotted spoon to kitchen paper.

Deep-fry the black pudding for 1 minute before removing to kitchen paper.

Skewer the mushrooms, black pudding and onion rings onto the slices of baguette before serving.

Serves: **8**   Preparation time: **15 minutes**   Cooking time: **20 minutes**

Strawberry Charlotte Style Cannelés

Ingredients

250 ml / 9 fl. oz / 1 cup double (heavy) cream

125 g / 4 ½ oz / 1 cup icing (confectioners') sugar

200 g / 7 oz / 2 cups strawberries, hulled and diced

30 ml / 1 fl. oz / 2 tbsp wild strawberry liqueur

30 ml / 1 fl. oz / 2 tbsp cold water

8 slices of white sandwich bread, crusts removed

1 lemon, juiced

Method

Toss the diced strawberries with half of the icing sugar in a mixing bowl.

Spoon into a colander sat over a mixing bowl and leave for 30 minutes at room temperature.

Add the strawberry liqueur, lemon juice and water to the accumulated liquid in the mixing bowl.

Cut the bread into strips and soak in the liquid before using to line the base and sides of 4 individual cannele moulds.

Reserve a few pieces of bread and some soaking liquid for the top of the Charlottes.

Whip the cream with the remaining icing sugar to soft peaks before folding through the strawberries.

Spoon into the cannele moulds, then soak the remaining pieces of bread and use as lids to cover the cream.

Cover the moulds and chill for at least 3 hours before turning out onto serving plates.

Makes: **4**   Preparation time: **10 minutes**   Cooking time: **15-20 minutes**

Rolled Sardines Marinated in Orange

Ingredients

6 sardine fillets, pin-boned

2 oranges, juiced

½ tsp coriander seeds, crushed

1 tbsp extra-virgin olive oil

1 orange, zest pared and finely sliced

Method

Whisk together the orange juice and coriander seeds in a mixing bowl.

Add the sardine fillets and mix well to coat evenly.

Cover the bowl with clingfilm and chill for at least 45 minutes.

Remove after chilling and allow the sardines to sit for 10 minutes before rolling and securing with cocktail sticks.

Serve on plates, drizzled with olive oil and garnished with orange zest.

Serves: **6**   Preparation time: **10-15 minutes**   Cooking time: **5 minutes**

Fig Shortbread Cookies

Ingredients

200 g / 7 oz / 1 ⅓ cups plain
(all purpose) flour

a little extra plain (all purpose) flour,
for dusting

150 g / 5 oz / ⅔ cup unsalted butter, cubed

65 g / 2 ½ oz / ½ cup icing
(confectioners') sugar

30 g / 1 oz / 2 tbsp cornflour (cornstarch)

30 g / 1 oz / 2 tbsp fennel seeds

4 figs

a pinch of salt

Method

Pulse together the flour, cornflour, salt, icing sugar and butter in a food processor until it comes together to form a dough.

Remove the dough, knead gently and form into a ball.

Wrap in clingfilm and chill for 60 minutes.

Preheat the oven to 180°C (160° fan) / 350F / gas 4.

Remove the ends of each fig then cut the remaining part of the fruit into 3 slices.

Grease and line 2 baking trays with greaseproof paper.

Remove the dough from the fridge and roll out on a lightly floured surface to ½ cm thickness.

Cut out 12 rounds from the dough using a fluted cookie cutter.

Arrange on the baking trays spaced apart and bake for 10-12 minutes until they just start to colour.

Remove from the oven and top each with a slice of fig, making sure the cut side is facing up.

Sprinkle with fennel seeds and return to the oven for 4-5 minutes.

Serves: **6**   Preparation time: **10 minutes**   Cooking time: **15-20 minutes**

Scallops with Red Wine Sauce

Ingredients

55 ml / 2 fl. oz / ¼ cup sunflower oil

6 scallops, roe removed

6 pleurotus mushrooms, brushed clean

250 ml / 9 fl. oz / 1 cup red wine

1 tsp caster (superfine) sugar

salt and pepper

6 sprigs of chervil leaves

Method

Reduce the wine in a saucepan until you are left with a thickened, syrupy liquid

Adjust the seasoning using the sugar, salt and pepper and keep warm to one s

Heat half of the oil in a frying pan set over a moderate heat until hot.

Season the mushrooms and pan-fry for 3-4 minutes until golden in colour.

Drain on kitchen paper and wipe the pan clean.

Add the remaining oil and heat until very hot.

Season the scallops on their tops and gently arrange in a circle in the oil on the seasoned side.

Season the unseasoned side of the scallops and flip onto that side after the undersides are golden in colour.

Cook for an additional 1-2 minutes on the other side depending on size; the scallops should be firm yet slightly springy to the touch.

Transfer to kitchen paper and rest for 1 minute.

Spoon the sauce into rimmed dishes, sit a scallop on it with a mushroom next t the scallop. Garnish with chervil before serving.

Serves: **6**   Preparation time: **5-10 minutes**   Cooking time: **15 minutes**

Brittany Lemon Tartlets

Ingredients

150 g / 5 oz / 1 cup plain (all purpose) flour

a little extra plain (all purpose) flour, for dusting

110 g / 4 oz / ½ cup good-quality salted butter, softened

110 g / 4 oz / ½ cup caster (superfine) sugar

1 small egg

½ tsp vanilla extract

30 ml / 1 fl. oz / 2 tbsp whole milk

225 g / 8 oz / 1 cup unsalted butter, softened

190 g / 6 ½ oz / 1 ½ cups icing (confectioners') sugar

2 lemons, juiced

a few lemon slices, halved

Method

Cream together the butter and sugar for the biscuits in a mixing bowl until pale and creamy.

Add the egg and vanilla and beat again briefly.

Add the flour, mix well, then turn the dough out onto a lightly floured surface.

Knead briefly before flattening, wrapping in clingfilm and chilling for 60 minutes.

Preheat the oven to 180°C (160° fan) / 350F / gas 4.

Roll the dough out to ¼ cm thickness and use a 2 inch straight-sided cookie cutter to stamp out 12 rounds.

Carefully lift onto a greaseproof paper-lined baking tray and brush with milk.

Bake for 12-15 minutes until deep golden-brown in colour.

Remove to a wire rack to cool.

Pulse the butter, icing sugar and lemon juice in a food processor until even and creamy.

Spoon into a piping bag fitted with a star-shaped nozzle and pipe onto the cooled biscuits.

Garnish with lemon slices before serving.

Serves: 4   Preparation time: **10 minutes**   Cooking time: **15-20 minutes**

Calamari Rings with Chorizo

Ingredients

2 frozen squid tubes, thawed

150 g / 5 oz / 1 cup chorizo, peeled

salt and pepper

1 tsp smoked paprika

a few chive stalks, finely chopped

Method

Preheat the grill to hot.

Stuff the squid tubes with the chorizo and cut into 1 inch thick slices.

Arrange flat on a lined baking tray and season a little.

Grill for 3-4 minutes until the chorizo is golden-brown and starting to crisp on top.

Remove from the grill and skewer with cocktail sticks.

Arrange on a serving plate and sprinkle with the smoked paprika and chives before serving.

Serves: **4**   Preparation time: **5-10 minutes**   Cooking time: **10 minutes**

INDEX